Postcard History Series

Sedona and Oak Creek Canyon

ON THE FRONT COVER: CATHEDRAL RED ROCK FORMATION, C. 1960. The Cathedral Rock formation is seen here from the back side, where a young boy is enjoying his time watching Oak Creek rush past in the area of Baldwin's Crossing. Cathedral Rock is one of the most photographed sites in Arizona and has become the most recognized icon of Sedona. (Published by Fronske Studio of Flagstaff, Arizona.)

ON THE BACK COVER: SLIDE ROCK, OAK CREEK CANYON, C. 1969. Slide Rock, now in Slide Rock State Park, is a natural waterslide in Oak Creek Canyon. From the top of the chute, the rushing water of Oak Creek carries a person over a series of rocks made slick by golden-brown algae and blue-green algae to a small pool at the bottom. People love sitting on the rocks on both sides of the slide to watch. (Published by Roben Company, Sedona, Arizona.)

POSTCARD HISTORY SERIES

Sedona and Oak Creek Canyon

Victoria L. Clark

Copyright © 2020 by Victoria L. Clark
ISBN 978-1-4671-0478-4

Published by Arcadia Publishing
Charleston, South Carolina

Library of Congress Control Number: 2019951554

For all general information contact Arcadia Publishing at:
Telephone 843-853-2070
Fax 843-853-0044
E-mail sales@arcadiapublishing.com
For customer service and orders:
Toll-Free 1-888-313-2665

Visit us on the Internet at www.arcadiapublishing.com

Dedicated to the farmers, ranchers, filmmakers, artists, photographers, entrepreneurs, US Forest Service personnel, and the many volunteers who have made Sedona the beautiful place that we are so lucky to call our home.

Contents

Acknowledgments		6
Introduction		7
1.	Sedona Has Four Seasons	9
2.	Early Residents, Farmers, and Ranchers	13
3.	Hollywood Comes to Sedona	25
4.	The Rocks Have Names	31
5.	The Town of Sedona Develops	41
6.	The Chapel of the Holy Cross	81
7.	Oak Creek Canyon	91
8.	Recreation Sedona Style	109
9.	Miscellaneous	121
Bibliography		127

Acknowledgments

I want to thank Janeen Trevillyan, president of the Sedona Heritage Museum Board, for encouraging me to share my collection of postcards by writing this book and for helping me find valuable research materials. I also want to thank the staff and volunteers at the Sedona Heritage Museum for maintaining excellent archives on the people and places of Sedona and Oak Creek Canyon. Their suggestions and knowledge were essential to my research. Kim Thompson, a friend and longtime resident, shared her memories and helped me with dating the postcard images, and another friend who grew up in Sedona, John Conway, helped me with his knowledge of filmmaking, early photographers, and area place names. I am always grateful for the postcard collectors and postcard dealers I have been privileged to know over the years for their knowledge of how to date and evaluate postcard types and images. As always, this book would not have happened without the kind encouragement of my husband, Mike; our daughters; and many wonderful friends.

All postcards are from my personal collection. For cards that list a publisher, the publisher's name is noted at the end of the caption as it appears on the postcard. Many of these publishers went by various similar-sounding names over time as studios were bought and sold and companies merged.

Any misconceptions or errors were not the author's intention.

INTRODUCTION

The history of Sedona is an amazing one, the story of how a tiny farming and ranching community became a travel destination for visitors from all over the world in a scant 100 years. If we could chart a time line, the prehistoric peoples discovered Verde Valley and settled to the south, west, and north of Sedona. Just like today, our first residents, the Native Americans, discovered four seasons of temperate weather and sources of abundant water and wildlife, which were their resources for survival. Necessity dictated that they create practical tools, clothing, and pottery, but from their petroglyphs, pottery designs, and other objects they created, they must have stood in awe of the giant red rock formations, the rushing water, and the variety of vegetation. They must have also appreciated the clear blue skies, the sunshine to grow their crops, and the dark skies to track the cycles of the moon and constellations at night.

Anglo pioneers began farming in the area in the late 1800s, and by 1902, T. Carl Schnebly applied for a post office. His first choice for a name for the settlement was Schnebly Station, but the story goes that the name was rejected as too long for a postal cancel. It was suggested that the community name should be Sedona in honor of T. Carl's wife. Farmers grew peaches, apples, plums, pears, grapes, and other fruits to feed their families and to sell to the nearby mining town of Jerome and the lumber camps near Flagstaff. Ranchers found good grazing areas around Sedona and then drove their cattle to be sold in Flagstaff.

When Hollywood began filming Westerns in the 1940s in Sedona and Oak Creek Canyon, film fans had a desire to see the area for themselves. The popularity of Western novels during this period also helped to create tourism. From those early tourists, word spread about the fantastic beauty of the red rock formations, the lush vegetation, the fishing, the hunting, and the horseback riding in Oak Creek Canyon. The former homesteads that had been settled by pioneer farmers and ranchers were purchased for cabins, motels, stores, restaurants, and service stations. Artists and writers began arriving, inspired by the beauty of the surroundings.

Sedona is governed by two counties, Coconino and Yavapai. The area along Arizona State Route 89A, called Uptown and adjacent to the entrance of lower Oak Creek Canyon, is an area of older houses, hotels, specialty shopping, galleries, restaurants, tourist activities, and views of Oak Creek. The area to the west of the junction of Route 89A and Arizona State Route 179 is called West Sedona and has a variety of housing areas, grocery stores, medical facilities, service stations, restaurants, movie theaters, schools, and the general variety of shopping and other services necessary in towns everywhere. One quirk in West Sedona is that the McDonald's there has the world's only teal-colored arches, to meet the requirement of Sedona's approved Southwestern paint scheme. To the south is the Village of Oak Creek on both sides of Route 179, which is a nice mix of housing, three golf courses, hotels, restaurants, service stations, and shopping.

Sedona is surrounded by 1.8 million acres of beautiful natural forestland, which serves to limit growth but has also meant higher prices for housing and the cost of living. The number of artists, writers, photographers, performers, and musicians living in Sedona continue to keep Sedona a vibrant community. The number of hiking trails and other outdoor activities range from strenuous to easy. The beauty of the red rocks still makes me catch my breath, even after living here full-time for the last 20 years, but other people must see what I see, since readers of the *USA Today* weekend edition once voted Sedona "America's Most Beautiful Place."

Since Sedona was primarily a farming and ranching community before the 1960s, postcards of the area were mainly limited to real-photo postcards credited to photographers and publishers outside Arizona. This changed during the 1950s when chrome color postcards became popular. After the 1950s, most of the Sedona and Oak Creek Canyon postcards were filmed and published by local area or other Arizona photographers. Many of Sedona's postcards are credited to local photographer Bob Bradshaw, who lived and worked in Sedona as a photographer, as a location scout for Western films, and as a part-time actor. Most of the early postcards were listed as located in Oak Creek Canyon rather than Sedona because the actual town of Sedona was so small. When tourism began fueling Sedona's growth during the 1960s, then postcard images were listed as being in Sedona. I hope you enjoy these beautiful postcards as much as I do.

One

Sedona Has Four Seasons

Spring—Peach Blossom Time at Call of the Canyon Resort Lodge, c. 1958.
Apples and peaches were two crops of prime importance in Sedona and Oak Creek Canyon. The fruit was sold in the surrounding towns of Flagstaff and Jerome and sometimes Phoenix. The spring temperatures in the area average a high of 72 and a low of 45, and many travel sites suggest that the best time to visit Sedona is during the months of March, April, or May. (Bob Petley Studios, Phoenix, Arizona.)

SUMMER—OAK CREEK CANYON IS A WONDERFUL PLACE FOR FISHING AND HUNTING, C. 1951. Fishing and hunting in Oak Creek has declined with the increase in population and number of visitors, but other outdoor sports such as hiking, trail biking, and driving off-road vehicles have increased. The average high temperature during the summer is 97, but 100 degrees is not unusual, and most summer nights average a pleasant 66 degrees. (Union Oil Company, Natural Scenes of the West, No. 92.)

SUMMER—OAK CREEK CANYON, C. 1966. The busiest time in Oak Creek Canyon is mid-summer, when most of Arizona is sweltering. Camping is very popular and requires advanced planning. The swimming holes and Slide Rock are crowded, but there are plenty of places for wading or splashing, hiking, or relaxing. (Bradshaw's Color Studios.)

FALL—RED MAPLE AND GOLDEN ASPENS ADD TO THE ENCHANTING COLORS OF OAK CREEK CANYON, C. 1958. September in Sedona often is a slightly cooler extension of summer, but in October, the weather begins cooling and the leaves begin to change colors. Temperatures range from highs of 74 to lows of 49. (Bob Bradshaw Photo Shop, Sedona, Arizona.)

WINTER—MISTLETOE OVER CATHEDRAL ROCK, C. 1965. When it snows, the red rock formations appear as giant frosted cakes. The town of Sedona averages about 9 to 11 inches of snow each year in most areas, which usually melts the next day. The higher elevations in Oak Creek Canyon receive more snow in the areas closer to Flagstaff. (Roben Company, Sedona, Arizona; photograph by Rollie F. Houck.)

WINTER—SLIDE ROCK STATE PARK, OAK CREEK CANYON, C. 1966. The summer crowds have gone from this popular natural waterslide in Slide Rock State Park, and the temperatures average 58 during the day and 33 at night. Oak Creek continues to flow year-round, and the Visitors Center remains open. (Bradshaw Color Studios, Sedona, Arizona.)

Two

EARLY RESIDENTS, FARMERS, AND RANCHERS

MONTEZUMA'S CASTLE, BUILT AROUND 1100 AD, C. 1940. Montezuma's Castle is in the Verde Valley, 11 miles from Sedona. Early explorers mistakenly thought the dwelling had been built by Aztec Indians from Mexico and named the ruin for Montezuma, an early Aztec ruler. Drawn by a year-round source of water and a temperate climate, the peaceful cliff-dwelling Native American farmers, believed to be the Southern Sinagua, hunted, gathered, and grew cotton, corn, beans, pumpkins, and squash, which were irrigated by canals from the nearby Beaver Creek. (E.C. Kropp Company, Milwaukee, Wisconsin.)

BEST PRESERVED PREHISTORIC CLIFF DWELLINGS IN THE UNITED STATES, C. 1955. Situated on a limestone cliff about 100 feet above the ground, this five-story structure with approximately 45 rooms housed an estimated 100 people. The residents created pottery and wove garments from the cotton they grew. Tools were formed from bones and stone. (Fronske Studio, Flagstaff, Arizona.)

MONTEZUMA CASTLE NATIONAL MONUMENT, C. 1968. Montezuma Castle was deserted around 1400, and where the inhabitants went and why remains a mystery. Some have suggested that they migrated north and merged with the Hopi tribe. The cliff dwellings were looted and damaged and continued to deteriorate until the area was declared a national monument. (Bradshaw Color Studios, Sedona, Arizona.)

MONTEZUMA WELL, NATURAL LIMESTONE SINK, C. 1957. The continuously flowing springs, approximately 55 feet deep, were used as a water source for the Sinagua cliff dwellers at Montezuma Castle and by those living in the surrounding smaller ruins and pit houses built around 1050 that surround the "Well." The irrigation ditches cut into the limestone remain viable today. (Dexter Press Natural Color; photograph by Bob Bradshaw.)

AERIAL VIEW OF MONTEZUMA WELL, C. 1958. Montezuma Well is a limestone sink surrounded by lush vegetation that might have been formed by the collapse of an underground cavern. The area supports a variety of waterfowl, water scorpions, muskrats, and Sonoran mud turtles, which are seen around the edge of the well. No fish can survive in the water, though, due to its limestone content. (Roben Company, Sedona Arizona.)

TUZIGOOT NATIONAL MONUMENT, C. 1958. Tuzigoot is an Apache term meaning "crooked water." The Sinagua pueblo ruins, built of mud, stone, and wood, sit high on a hill not far from the Verde River. Various Native American farmers, artists, and traders lived there from 1100 to 1400, then disappeared. The amount of jewelry and other crafts found suggests that the residents had some leisure time. Several theories about their disappearance include warfare, disease, or famine. (Color King Natural Color, Chattanooga, Tennessee.)

AERIAL VIEW OF TUZIGOOT RUIN, C. 1960. The fortified hilltop pueblo is believed to have been two stories in places, with 110 rooms. Access to the rooms was through holes in the roofs by ladders. Pres. Franklin Delano Roosevelt declared Tuzigoot a national monument in 1939. (Bradshaw Color Studios, Sedona, Arizona.)

TUZIGOOT GROUND FLOOR RUINS, C. 1966. The ruins extended 500 feet along the north-south ridge. The Mingus Mountains are seen in the background. In front of the ruins was fertile farming land. Tuzigoot's source of water was the Verde River, 120 feet below. (Bradshaw Color Studios, Sedona, Arizona.)

TUZIGOOT VISITOR CENTER AND MUSEUM, C. 1968. The visitor center was built by the Works Progress Administration to house artifacts unearthed during the excavation of the ruins in 1933–1934. Today, it offers information on two self-guided short loop walks, bird walks, field trips, and a bookstore. (Dobie Graphics, Cornville, Arizona.)

PENDLEY RANCH, OAK CREEK CANYON, REAL-PHOTO POSTCARD, C. 1945. The Pendleys arrived in Oak Creek to homestead and built their house in 1907. Later, they added a few tourist cabins. They planted apple and peach orchards, which they watered by hand from Oak Creek until they built an irrigation system. The system was made by blasting through rock to create tunnels and adding a flume to carry water from Oak Creek. The orchard was best known for its varieties of apples, which included red delicious, Stagman winesaps, and Arkansas blacks. (Publisher unidentified.)

THE CHAVEZ RANCH, C. 1962. The Ambrosio Chavez Ranch was established by his parents in 1902. A homestead claim was filed in 1909. The apple orchard was irrigated by water from Oak Creek, which flows year-round. A family member recalled that the apples were also made into applejack or cider vinegar to sell in Flagstaff. (Bob Bradshaw Photo Shop, Sedona, Arizona.)

FAMOUS CATHEDRAL ROCK SCENE, C. 1966. Cathedral Rock provides a colorful backdrop for the people and horses in this peaceful ranch scene. The ranch house was constructed of local red rocks, and the outbuilding was a board-and-batten style to utilize local building materials that were inexpensive and readily available. Materials from abandoned buildings were recycled and used. (Petley Studios, Phoenix, Arizona.)

COLORFUL FORMATIONS AND CATTLE GRAZING, REAL-PHOTO POSTCARD, C. 1947. This scene is in the area of West Sedona today. Note Coffee Pot Rock in the background; the location written on the card is incorrect. Oak Creek Canyon does not go from Flagstaff to Prescott, but at the time this photograph was taken, most people did not know where Oak Creek or Sedona were. (Frasher's Fotos, Pomona, California.)

CATTLE DRIVE ON SCHNEBLY HILL ROAD, C. 1965. Cattle raised in the Sedona area were driven to Flagstaff on trails such as Munds Trail (later Schnebly Hill Road) and Casner Trail to be loaded on trains. A roundup to move the cattle required many cowboys and horses, so most ranchers would help each other. (Bradshaw's Photo Shop, Sedona, Arizona.)

OAK CREEK CANYON—CATTLE COUNTRY, C. 1965. White-faced Hereford cattle quench their thirst in a water catch cattle pond in Sedona. In the winter months, many ranchers from areas north of Oak Creek Canyon moved their herds to the Sedona area, and if a summer was dry, cattle were moved to areas north of Sedona to graze. (Bradshaw Distributing Company, Sedona, Arizona.)

CATTLE COUNTRY, OAK CREEK CANYON, C. 1967. Cowboys herd cattle through the spectacular red rock formations 30 miles south of Flagstaff on Route 89A. Most ranchers did not own large tracts of land, and relied on permits from the US Forest Service for grazing. (Dexter Press Inc., New York.)

OLD ADOBE HUT AND PINON LOG CORRAL, OAK CREEK CANYON, C. 1968. The adobe hut and pinon pine log corral fence on this ranch were typical and inexpensive. By the end of the 1960s, cattle ranching was rapidly diminishing as the population and tourism were increasing. (Bob Petley Studios, Phoenix, Arizona.)

DUDE RANCHES ABOUND ALL OVER THE WEST, C. 1941. Dude ranches were once plentiful in the West, particularly in Arizona. Here, riders gaze at red rock formation in Sedona. The ranches advertised horseback riding, hunting, fishing, and just plain resting. (Union Oil Company, Natural Color Scenes of the West, California.)

Three

HOLLYWOOD COMES TO SEDONA

THE SEDONA LODGE, C. 1957. Sedona Lodge was constructed in 1946 by the Anderson Boarding and Supply Company, which normally built logging and mining camps. Built on the former site of a Civilian Conservation Corps camp, Sedona Lodge was used to house film crews and their animals and equipment. Being so close to the filming locations was a huge advantage. The bungalows were able to house 150 people. A sound stage with two sets, a recreation hall, dining hall, office, swimming pool, and a barn for horses and other animals made Sedona Lodge a unique place. When filming was not in progress, the bungalows were rented to tourists. The property was sold in 1958. Some of the bungalows were sold individually and moved to locations around Verde Valley, but the remaining buildings were torn down and King's Ransom Inn was constructed on the site. (Bradshaw's Photo Shop, Sedona, Arizona.)

MAYHEW'S OAK CREEK LODGE, C. 1958. *Call of the Canyon,* a silent film, was based on Zane Grey's novel of the same name. It is credited with being the first film made in Oak Creek Canyon, but some claim that another silent film was made in the same location as early as 1918. Scenes from *Call of the Canyon* were filmed at Mayhew's Oak Creek Lodge and the nearby West Fork hiking trail. *Riders of the Purple Sage,* also from a novel by Zane Grey, was filmed in Sedona in 1931. The dramatic landscape and the temperate climate made the area attractive for film companies. (Dexter Press Inc., West Nayack, New York.)

LITTLE HORSE PARK, C. 1956. Little Horse Park was the site of the original Cole-White Cattle Co. Ranch. It was later chosen to be the location of the Quirt Ranch in the film *Angel and the Badman,* starring John Wayne and Gail Russell. The film was Wayne's debut as a producer. Full-scale sets of barns, houses, and corrals were built in this area but later torn down. Directors often were quoted as saying that they loved filming in Sedona because the scenery was interesting in every direction. They also usually commented on the helpfulness and friendliness of the community. (Lollesgard Specialty, Phoenix, Arizona.)

OLD MOVIE STREET, SEDONA, ARIZONA, C. 1957. This Western street set was built for Republic Films in West Sedona under Coffee Pot Rock for the filming of *Angel and the Badman*. The set included saloons, a bank, a hotel, a stagecoach depot, and a train depot. It was modified several times for use in other Western films. Over 60 full-length feature films were made in Oak Creek Canyon and Sedona, but the first time a movie company agreed to use the name Sedona rather than Oak Creek Canyon as the location was not until 1964 in *Rounders*, with Glenn Ford and Henry Fonda. (Petley Studios, Phoenix, Arizona.)

WESTERN STREET MOVIE SET, C. 1957. When not in use, tourists loved taking pictures of the "town" and each other on the set. Several community events in Sedona were held here. The last time the set was used in a film was the original version of *310 to Yuma*, starring Glenn Ford and Felicia Farr in 1957. The set was torn down in 1959 for a housing development, and the streets were named for films made in Sedona. (Petley Studios, Phoenix, Arizona.)

FALLS IN OAK CREEK CANYON, C. 1958. These few feet of rushing water in Oak Creek Canyon were used as dangerous rapids in early Westerns. By 1950, approximately 500 residents lived in the Sedona/Oak Creek area, but Western films had created such a longing to see red rock country that tourists and new residents began arriving. By the mid-1960s, one film executive rightly noted that there were now too many red-roofed houses to film Westerns here. (Fronske Studio, Flagstaff, Arizona.)

FROM SCHNEBLY HILL, C. 1964. Schnebly Hill Road began as a narrow cattle trail made by rancher William Munds. It was built by various pioneer families as a wagon route to deliver produce to Flagstaff. Instead of having to travel miles around the sheer canyon walls and red rock formations, the road allowed travel from near present-day Tlaquepaque to the top of the Mogollon Rim. Film crews discovered that the winding dirt road offered spectacular views of lower Oak Creek Canyon and was a perfect, but dangerous, place for runaway wagons, like in *Angel and the Badman*. (Bradshaw Distributing Company, Sedona, Arizona.)

MOVIEMAKING IN SEDONA, C. 1958. When Western films required Native Americans, they were brought to Sedona from northern Arizona tribes. During the filming of *Broken Arrow*, 250 White Mountain Apaches were hired. Extras were paid $15 to $45 per day. According to Bob Bradshaw, a local photographer who helped film companies scout locations and sometimes acted as a double or extra in the films, extras in Westerns usually rode on solid-colored horses of black or brown, so that the main actors, who were given "fancy" horses, would stand out. (Bradshaw's Color Studios, Sedona, Arizona.)

MOVIE INDIANS, C. 1957. Toward the end of the popularity of Westerns, Joe McNeill stated in *Arizona's Little Hollywood: Sedona and Northern Arizona's Forgotten Film History* that it was getting increasingly hard to find Indians who had not cut their hair or still wore traditional tribal dress. He also lamented that it was harder to find open areas without buildings or poles. (Bradshaw Photo Shop, Sedona, Arizona.)

APACHE ON HORSEBACK, C. 1960. The Sedona film *Broken Arrow*, starring Jimmy Stewart as Tom Jeffords, was one of the first to recognize injustice to Native Americans. One of the worst films ever made in Sedona was *Stay Away Joe*. Elvis Presley starred as a half-breed who returns home. The script portrayed Native Americans as lazy and immoral, and Presley was reduced to singing to a bull. The film was understandably criticized and panned. (Dexter Press, West Nyack, New York.)

Four

THE ROCKS HAVE NAMES

CASTLE ROCK, OAK CREEK, ARIZONA, REAL-PHOTO POSTCARD, C. 1949. Today, this beautiful four-spire red rock formation is called Cathedral Rock, but for years, the names of the rocks have been debated by the residents of Sedona. This formation, one of the best known, is widely used as the icon for Sedona and is seen in many films made in the area as well in print advertising and television commercials. The front side of the formation can be seen off Route 179 near the Chapel area, and on the back side is Baldwin's Crossing, currently called Red Rock Crossing. It appears that the residents are still debating what the "real" names of the rocks and areas surrounding Sedona are. (Publisher unidentified.)

A Pair of Beauties at Baldwin's Crossing, c. 1968. This area behind Cathedral Rock is one of the most photographed sites in Arizona. A popular way to hike to Cathedral Rock is a trail off Back and Beyond Road. One of the questions that many people ask is, "What makes the red rocks red?" A simple answer is that each grain of Supai sandstone is coated with red iron oxide. (Publisher unidentified.)

Steamboat or Battleship Rock, c. 1958. This impressive formation can be seen north of Uptown, near Midgely Bridge. From a distance, the red rock formations appear solid, but on a closer inspection, there are layers of buff-colored sandstone and white sandstone and often a layer of dark lava. (Roben Company, Sedona, Arizona; photograph by Rollie F. Houck.)

COFFEE POT ROCK, C. 1964. This formation used to be easily recognized as an old percolator coffee pot, but with the advent of so many types of modern drip and pod coffee makers, younger people have trouble seeing it as anything related to coffee. (Bradshaw Distributing Company, Sedona, Arizona.)

COFFEE POT ROCK, C. 1940. The Coffee Pot Rock formation is in West Sedona. It has rich red coloration and is dotted with green pines. While many of the rock formation names have changed over time, Coffee Pot Rock was referenced by Sedona pioneer Don Bell as early as 1903. (Union Oil Company, California.)

CHIMNEY ROCK, REAL-PHOTO POSTCARD, C. 1949. Chimney Rock is two spires, although it appears to be one formation when viewed from the front. Most tourists to Sedona say that the main reason they came was to see the giant red rock formations in the area. One visitor asked a volunteer at the Sedona Visitor Center, "What time do the Red Rocks open?" (Publisher unidentified.)

HARDING'S PIPE ORGAN, OAK CREEK CANYON, ARIZONA, REAL-PHOTO POSTCARD, C. 1948. Wind and water and other forces of nature carved all the red rock formations, yet they have very different shapes and sizes. Since Arizona was covered with water 300 to 400 million years ago, fossils can be found in the red rocks. (Publisher unidentified.)

BELL ROCK, C. 1960. Bell Rock was one site of the Harmonic Convergence, World Harmony Day, when seven planets aligned between August 14 and 20, 1987. An estimated 1,800 people waited around Bell Rock, which was said to contain an energy vortex, where some believed a spaceship would land or the whales trapped inside would emerge or a light in the shape of a cross would appear. (Bradshaw Photo Shop, Sedona, Arizona.)

ALONG THE WAY OF TWA, OAK CREEK CANYON, C. 1950. This may be the most unusual postcard in this book because Transcontinental and Western Airlines (later Trans World Airlines or TWA) did not fly into Sedona; the area did not have an airport capable of handling airliners. Jack Frye, president and cofounder of TWA, and his wife, Helen, purchased a 700-acre ranch in the area that is Red Rock State Park today. Bell Rock is on the left, and Courthouse Rock is on the right. The area in front of the rock formations is now the village of Oak Creek. (Publisher unidentified.)

CLIFFS IN LOWER OAK CREEK CANYON, ARIZONA, REAL-PHOTO POSTCARD, C. 1949.
Pictured is the Rooster Comb or Cock's Comb formation. It is easy to see the alternate layers of red, buff, and white sandstone. Depending on the time of day or the amount of cloud cover, the layers and holes created by wind and erosion make the rocks appear different. (Publisher unidentified.)

THE FOUR NUNS OR CHICKEN FEET, C. 1965. The Four Nuns or Chicken Feet are the four spires on the right. Four Nuns is the most popular name since the Chapel of the Holy Cross was built to the left of this formation. The name Chicken Feet makes sense only when looking at the bottom of the two spires at right. (Petley Studios, Phoenix, Arizona.)

LITTLE HORSE PARK, REAL-PHOTO POSTCARD, C. 1949. Once part of a ranch, this land was a popular backdrop for several early Western films. The Chicken Feet or Four Nuns are at right. While a popular hiking trail still retains the name Little Horse, today the area surrounding the rock is a housing development called Chapel Hills. (Publisher unidentified.)

MERRY-GO-ROUND ROCK ENERGY VORTEX CIRCLES, C. 1964. Merry-Go-Round Rock is about five miles up Schnebly Hill Road. The formation was referenced in a 1901 account by Sedona pioneer Albert E. Thompson in his account of blasting and creating Schnebly Hill Road. Merry-Go-Round Rock is a popular place for weddings, where the bride and groom stand at the top. The smaller, flat, circular-shaped formations are believed by New Age followers to be places of a special creative and healing energy. (Bob Petley, Phoenix, Arizona.)

MADONNA OF THE ROCKS, C. 1969. A natural red rock formation near the Chapel of the Holy Cross appears as the Madonna holding baby Jesus. Marguerite Brunswig Staude said that the Madonna was one of the signs that showed her Sedona was the correct area for her to build the Chapel of the Holy Cross. (Tichnor Brothers, Boston, Massachusetts; photograph by Howard Houck.)

GRAY MOUNTAIN, OAK CREEK CANYON, REAL-PHOTO POSTCARD, C. 1949. This large formation is called Sugar Loaf today, and the area once known as Grasshopper Flats is a very populated place in West Sedona. (Publisher unidentified.)

Five

THE TOWN OF SEDONA DEVELOPS

SCHNEBLY HILL ROAD, OAK CREEK CANYON, ARIZONA, REAL-PHOTO POSTCARD, C. 1948. In 1902, Sedona was officially established when T. Carl Schnebly applied for a post office for the 70 families living in the area. Schnebly named the town for his wife. Several pioneer families worked on this road, formerly named the Verde Cut-Off Road, as a shortcut to Flagstaff. Schnebly Hill Road begins at the roundabout where Route 179 intersects with Oak Creek and winds to 7,000 feet at the top, where it joins Interstate 17. The views of Sedona and Oak Creek Canyon from Schnebly Hill Road are fantastic. (Publisher unidentified.)

1930s CCC Camp F-32A, Sedona, Arizona, Real-Photo Postcard, c. 1940. At first, the camp was just tents, but this image shows barrack-like buildings. Approximately 311 men worked on projects for the US Forest Service in Oak Creek Canyon and around Verde Valley. Their projects included forestry, bridges, and a barn at the ranger station. (Frashers Fotos, Pomona, California.)

Hart's Store, Sedona, Arizona, Real-Photo Postcard, c. 1948. "Dad" Hart established this general store around 1913, which at the time was on the main road through Sedona. Later, he expanded from groceries and other supplies and added gasoline. (Frashers Fotos, Pomona, California.)

WILSON MOUNTAIN AND BATTLESHIP ROCK, C. 1952. Cattle graze in an open field, and a few structures can be seen. Wilson Mountain was named for Richard Wilson, who claimed to be a bear hunter from Arkansas. He was hired by Jim Thompson to help on Thompson's farm in Indian Gardens, but never arrived. Eight days later, he was discovered dead, having been mauled by a bear on a mountain near where Midgley Bridge would later be built. (Bradshaw's Color Studios.)

AERIAL VIEW OF SEDONA, ARIZONA, C. 1958. This aerial view shows Sedona with Highways 89A and 179 meeting at the area called "the Y." The Matterhorn Motor Lodge and other businesses along Route 89A and the George Jordan farm and Walter Jordan orchards can be seen. Sedona is described on this postcard as a "thriving little town" 33 miles south of Flagstaff. (Petley Studios, Phoenix, Arizona.)

AERIAL VIEW OF SEDONA, ARIZONA, C. 1964. This was taken from approximately the same location as the 1958 aerial view on the previous page. Both were taken by Bob Petley. Note the amount of new development along Highways 179 and 89A, although the card still describes Sedona as just a "thriving little town" 33 miles south of Flagstaff. (Petley Studios, Phoenix, Arizona.)

DEVELOPMENT ALONG ROUTE 89A, C. 1960. This area along Route 89A under Coffee Pot Rock shows the development of businesses in West Sedona. Wilson Mountain is in the background at right. (Petley Studios, Phoenix, Arizona.)

THE HITCHING POST MOTEL AND CAFÉ, C. 1950. The back of this card reads, "Deluxe accommodations and fine food in the dining room, in the heart of America's most beautiful scenery. AAA approved." The phone number listed was Sedona 9. The American Automobile Association (AAA) rated and approved lodgings, restaurants, and other places of interest to travelers. (Bradshaw Color Roundup, Sedona, Arizona.)

THE HITCHING POST MOTEL, C. 1954. This motel was first built in 1945 on Route 89A for tourists. Note that flagstone has replaced the earlier wooden siding, and Western details such as the wagon wheels have been added along with more units, as the town hoped to capitalize on the popularity of the Western films being made in Sedona. (Tichnor Gloss Card, Washington, DC.)

HITCHING POST RESTAURANT, C. 1962. The front of the restaurant has been updated again, and a modern neon sign has been added on the rooftop. A Bell telephone sign and phone booth are at left. (Bradshaw Color Studios, Sedona, Arizona.)

HITCHING POST MOTEL, C. 1962. A neon horse was added to the Hitching Post Motel sign as well as outdoor tables with umbrellas. A 1959 or 1960 Thunderbird sits at right. The owners at this time were listed as Jim and Grace Baker, and the phone number had changed to five digits. (Bradshaw Color Studios, Sedona, Arizona.)

HITCHING POST RESTAURANT, C. 1973. The Hitching Post Restaurant was updated several times since 1946 and relocated to a new building when the original restaurant and motel were torn down. While the restaurant changed its name to HP, it is still known for its homemade pies. The interior maintains its Western decor. (Both, Bradshaw Color Studios, Sedona, Arizona.)

GREETINGS FROM SEDONA, ARIZONA, C. 1964. Pictured here is a split view of Uptown Sedona. The top image shows development along Route 89A, including the sign for Oak Creek Market and Tavern, which opened in 1945. The Oak Creek Tavern is famous for the four cowboy artists—Joe Beeler, George Phippen, Charlie Dye, and John Hampton—who met there in 1965 to form the Cowboy Artists of America. They wanted to promote the American West and the lifestyle of cowboys. The bottom image shows the housing area behind the Matterhorn Motor Lodge. (Bradshaw Distributing Company, Sedona, Arizona.)

MOTELS, RESTAURANTS, AND HOUSES, C. 1956. Looking south on Route 89A, a few horses can be seen in the open space at lower left. However, development is increasing, and horses would not be corralled in town much longer. (Lolisgard Specialty Co., Phoenix, Arizona.)

TOURISM, ARTISTS, AND LAND SALES, C. 1956. Pictured here are the Hitching Post Motel and the Bradshaw Photo Shop with its Kodak Film sign on the west side of Route 89A. Note the large real estate office at left. (Fronske Studio, Flagstaff, Arizona.)

SEDONA LOOKING NORTH TOWARD OAK CREEK CANYON, C. 1956. This image shows both sides of Route 89A. A Sherwin Williams Paints hardware store sign hangs above the trucks at right. Several vintage pickup trucks indicate that farming or ranching were still common in the area. Battleship Rock is in the background. (Petley Studios, Phoenix, Arizona.)

SEDONA, ARIZONA, C. 1957. A couple of men fill up at the Canyon Portal Shell service station. Both a gas pump sign and a pickup truck, to the left of the Shell sign, advertise Goodyear tires. The service station also sold gifts, sporting goods, and fishing supplies and licenses. Enjoy the variety of 1950s cars. (Dexter Press Inc., West Nyack, New York.)

GREETINGS FROM SEDONA, ARIZONA, C. 1965. A vacation, retirement, and artist community, Sedona is located in the red rock area of northern Arizona. The area's elevation is 4,300 feet. (Roben Company, Sedona, Arizona.)

SUNSET COURT, C. 1955. One mile west of Sedona on Route 89A, the modern cabins at Sunset Court were the perfect spot to stay for trips to Flagstaff, the Grand Canyon, Montezuma Castle, and the Tuzigoot ruins. (Dexter Press Inc., West Nyack, New York.)

SUNSET COURT, C. 1962. This motel had modern cabins, some with kitchenettes. The Sunset Court was quiet and restful, and its owners were Ted and Hallie Lutz. (Dexter Press Inc., West Nyack, New York.)

RAY MEANY'S SUNSET MOTEL, C. 1968. Pictured are Coffee Pot Rock and Wilson Mountain with the renamed Sunset Motel (former Sunset Court) and gift shop. Guests are relaxing in the motel's metal chairs. The motel was renamed again to the Crimson Cliffs Motel in August 1971. (Bradshaw's Color Studios, Sedona, Arizona.)

WAGON WHEEL MOTEL AND CAFÉ, C. 1967. The Wagon Wheel Motel and Café is 22 miles south of Flagstaff on Route 89A, on Oak Creek Star Route in Oak Creek Canyon. (Bradshaw's Color Studios, Sedona, Arizona.)

THE VUE MOTEL AND ANTIQUE SHOP, C. 1964. The Vue was on the north end of Sedona, just a few steps from Oak Creek. It had large three-room housekeeping units available, and an antique store inside the lobby. Willard and Katherine Hardcastle were the owners. (Bradshaw Photo Shop, Sedona, Arizona.)

LOWER END OF OAK CREEK CANYON, SEDONA, ARIZONA, C. 1968. A mix of shops and services along Route 89A is seen here. Note the signs for the Sedona Pharmacy (a "Walgreen Agency"), a café, the Frontier Shop, a utility company, Oak Creek Market, Oak Creek Tavern, and an Enco service station. (Arizona Pictures, Sedona, Arizona.)

CEDAR MOTEL, OAK CREEK CANYON, C. 1968. Located at the junction of Highways 179 and 89A overlooking Oak Creek, the Cedar Motel was expanded and updated in 1964. Some units had kitchenettes that came completely equipped with everything guests would need.

CREEK CANYON

According to photographer and longtime resident Bob Bradshaw, who created this card, red rock country is a photographer's paradise, with fishing, swimming, sightseeing, and hiking. (Bradshaw's Color Studios, Sedona, Arizona.)

CEDARS RESORT, C. 1979. Formerly the Cedar Motel, this building was updated and the name changed to Cedars Resort. It continues to operate in the same location. (Mitchell Color Cards, Petoskey, Michigan.)

SILVER SPRUCE AND VAGABOND HOUSE CURIOS AND GIFTS, C. 1958. Looking south in Sedona in the heart of red rock country, the Silver Spruce café, "Home of Homemade Bread," can be seen. The Vagabond House gift shop is right next door. (Petley Studios, Phoenix, Arizona.)

VAGABOND HOUSE CURIOS AND GIFTS AND FREE PHOTOGRAPH TOWER, C. 1966. The Vagabond House sold both local Western and imported gifts. The owners encouraged visitors to use the "Free Photo Tower" to photograph the majestic views. A sign for the Silver Spruce café is at right, in front of the Matterhorn Motor Lodge. (Bradshaw Photos, Sedona, Arizona.)

MATTERHORN MOTOR LODGE, C. 1959. The Matterhorn Motor Lodge, built by A.K. Ragle in 1957 in Oak Creek Canyon, had AAA approval, a heated pool, air conditioning, and a view from every room. (Bradshaw's Photo Studios, Sedona, Arizona.)

MATTERHORN MOTOR LODGE, C. 1966. Note the changes from the previous image. A silver spruce tree has been planted next to the former Silver Spruce café, which has changed its name to the Silver Spruce Restaurant. The Matterhorn sign has been updated, and houses have been built next to the water tower in the background. By 1966, in conjunction with Northern Arizona University, students and artists were involved in instructional activities at the nearby Sedona Arts Center and the Sedona Art Barn, formerly the George Jordan packing shed. The center is still located across Route 89A close to the Matterhorn Motor Lodge. (Bradshaw's Color Studios, Sedona, Arizona.)

POOL SCENE AT THE MATTERHORN MOTOR LODGE, C. 1965. Visitors to the Matterhorn are enjoying the pool and sunshine around 1965. The pool area still looks very much like this postcard. (Bradshaw's Color Studios, Sedona Arizona.)

MATTERHORN MOTOR LODGE, C. 1979. The original turquoise of the Matterhorn was replaced with City of Sedona–approved colors of rust and brown. In addition to the Matterhorn's AAA rating, it had also received a Friendship Inns of America membership by this time. (Horizons West, Flagstaff, Arizona.)

SEDONA, ARIZONA, C. 1968. The top image looks north toward Battleship Rock on Route 89A. The bottom image shows the area once known as the Y, where Route 179 intersected with 89A to West Sedona or Uptown Sedona. (Bradshaw Distributing Company, Sedona, Arizona.)

WAYSIDE CHAPEL, C. 1967. The Wayside Chapel, an interdenominational church, was built in 1949 and dedicated on April 5, 1950. The chapel was not only built for the community of Sedona, but was intentionally placed on the side of Route 89A as a place for travelers to stop and worship or to sit a moment to reflect. The bell in the tower was donated by the Schnebly family as a memorial to Sedona Schnebly, who had requested that it be rung each day at noon. The chapel has been upgraded but remains at the same location in Uptown Sedona. (Bradshaw's Color Studios, Sedona, Arizona.)

ARLING-SMITH REALTY, POST OFFICE PLAZA, C. 1970. Arling-Smith Realty advertised, "For all real estate needs: Lots, Homes, Acreage, Commercial or Investment." (Bradshaw's Color Studios, Sedona, Arizona.)

BROOKHAVEN, C. 1960. Brookhaven was a vacation paradise in Sedona complete with modern units and cottages. The name later changed to Red Rock Lodge, and then to Lomacasi. It was a perfect place to swim, hike, take pictures, or relax. The motel's advertising stated that it was the "Wonderland of the West." (Both, Bradshaw's Photo Shop, Sedona, Arizona.)

HAWKEYE TRAILER PARK AND SUPPLIES, C. 1969. This trailer park was at the north end of Uptown Sedona with access to Oak Creek. Later, the property was purchased by the ILX Resort Corporation. (Publisher unidentified.)

CRIMSON CLIFFS INDIAN ARTS AND CRAFTS, C. 1969. As visitors and residents became familiar with the Native American arts of the Southwest, there was a greater demand for Navajo rugs, sand paintings, jewelry, pottery, fetishes, and kachinas. This shop was owned by Tom and Shirley McCune and was located at Route 89A and Airport Road. (Bradshaw's Color Studios, Sedona, Arizona.)

The Eagle Dancer

THE EAGLE DANCER INDIAN ARTS AND CRAFTS, C. 1969. The Eagle Dancer, "Located in the Husberg's Fine Arts Building," sold "Indian arts and crafts of the finest quality." Many tourists come to Sedona wanting to buy quality Native American arts and crafts, and there are still many places that sell authentic pieces of the finest quality, but a working knowledge of the artist, knowing the reputation of the seller, or the average price of similar pieces is always a good idea. (Roben Company, Sedona, Arizona.)

SCULPTURED ARTS, C. 1979. Sculptured Arts was in the Tlaquepaque Arts and Crafts Village on Route 179. So many artists were living in Sedona that both art galleries and the reputations of the artists flourished. (Horizons West, Flagstaff, Arizona.)

CANYON PORTAL MOTEL, C. 1946. Located on Route 89A on the east side of Uptown Sedona, the Canyon Portal Motel was built between 1945 and 1946 by Don and Ruth Willard. The cast of *Broken Arrow*, including Jimmy Stewart and Jeff Chandler, stayed here during filming. (Arthur J. Merrill, Taos, New Mexico.)

CANYON PORTAL MOTEL, C. 1950. "It's a wonderful climate and a delightful place to rest and relax. It's a friendly country," read an advertisement for the motel. In 1970, ten new units were added, and in 1987, the motel expanded again, adding spaces for tour buses. (Color Roundup Photo Shop, Sedona, Arizona.)

CANYON PORTAL MOTEL—SEDONA, ARIZONA IN BEAUTIFUL OAK CREEK CANYON, c. 1979. The original single-story motel was torn down to create 51 new rooms and 17,250 feet of retail space in Uptown Sedona. Each room had a king- or queen-sized bed and a private deck

Sedona, Arizona
Creek Canyon

with views of Oak Creek. The motel also had a gift shop, and the reservation desk offered to arrange area tours for guests. (Bradshaw's Color Studios, Sedona, Arizona.)

VILLAGE INN MOTEL, C. 1969. The Village Inn Motel was on the west side of Route 179, between Tlaquepaque and the Ranch House Restaurant. The motel underwent a dramatic remodel in 2018 and changed its name to Sedona Hill Top Inn. The location is very close to Tlaquepaque, restaurants, and shopping, and has wonderful views of Camel's Head and Snoopy Rock formations. (Bradshaw's Color Studios, Sedona, Arizona.)

STAR MOTEL, C. 1973. Built by owner Tony Gnader and his wife, this motel opened as the Northern Star Motel in 1961 on Jordon Road in Uptown Sedona. Current guests rave about its location in Uptown as they have parking and can walk everywhere. (Publisher unidentified.)

RONDEE MOTOR HOTEL, C. 1969. A three-level motel with an incomparable view of Oak Creek Canyon, the Rondee featured television and phones in every room. It was a Best Western affiliate and had AAA approval. (Petley Studios, Phoenix, Arizona.)

RONDEE MOTOR HOTEL, C. 1969. The Rondee's rooms were done in earth tones and had a hanging light on a chain and chairs on the balcony for viewing Oak Creek and Oak Creek Canyon. The Rondee was purchased in 1985 and is currently part of L'Auberge Resort. (Petley Studios, Phoenix, Arizona.)

THE TURTLE RESTAURANT, C. 1979. The Turtle restaurant and cocktail lounge opened in June 1962. The name was chosen to encourage people to "slow down and live a little." The draperies were handwoven by Mary Pendleton, owner of the Pendleton Shop on Jordan Road. The restaurant was part of the Rondee Motor Hotel on Route 89A in the center of Uptown Sedona and was owned by Mr. and Mrs. Henry Critten and managed by "Stretch" and Elsie Malden, who also managed the Silver Spruce Restaurant just north of the Turtle. (Bradshaw's Color Studios, Sedona, Arizona.)

EAST SIDE OF HIGHWAY 89A, SEDONA, ARIZONA, C. 1966. Looking west from Route 89A are the back of the Rondee Motor Hotel at left and the front of the Matterhorn Motor Lodge at right. The card references Sedona as the home of many famous artists and writers and as the place where the 1964 MGM movie *Rounders* was filmed. This might have been because locals hoped that the success of that movie would encourage other film companies to return to Sedona. (Roben Company, Sedona, Arizona.)

RED-CARPET RESTAURANT, C. 1968. Several longtime residents have stated they believe this restaurant was in West Sedona at the La Pasada Center, where Judi's restaurant is currently. The owners were Dick and June Duncan, but no address was stated on the card. Throughout the years, the Duncans owned several restaurants in Sedona, including the Hitching Post, the Chipmunk Lodge, Rainbow's End Restaurant and Lounge, and the Poco Diablo Restaurant and Lounge. (Bradshaw's Color Studios, Sedona, Arizona.)

MEYER'S HIDEAWAY DELICATESSEN RESTAURANT, C. 1958. Located on Route 179, this restaurant is still in business and has beautiful views from its balcony, which overlooks Oak Creek and several stunning red rock formations. (Roben Company, Sedona, Arizona.)

DUTCHMAN'S COVE RESTAURANT, C. 1969. Dutchman's Cove opened on April 4, 1969, below the Sedona Art Barn on the banks of Oak Creek. The restaurant specialized in steaks, prime rib, and seafood. It advertised elegant dining and cocktails. Each table had a view overlooking the cool waters of Oak Creek. Note the glass ashtray on the table for smoking. (Bob Clemenz Photography, Sedona, Arizona.)

SUGAR LOAF LODGE, C. 1978. The Sugar Loaf Lodge is at 1870 West Highway 89A in West Sedona. This small lodge offers a beautiful view of Sugar Loaf Mountain, located behind the lodge. (Publisher unidentified.)

PENDLETON SHOP, C. 1973. The Pendleton Shop opened on February 2, 1964, at 407 Jordan Road. The store sold top-quality looms and wools, and owner Mary Pendleton offered classes in spinning, hand weaving, and vegetal dyeing. Pendleton and her husband, Fred, also owned an arts and crafts store in the Tlaquepaque Arts and Crafts Village and were the publishers of *The Looming Arts*, a publication for hand weavers. (Horizons West, Flagstaff, Arizona.)

CANYON VIEW APARTMENTS ON LITTLE BIRD LANE, C. 1970. A.B. Pyle was the proprietor of these nicely furnished one and two bedroom apartments. They were near churches, shopping, and a medical center, and the rates were reasonable. These apartments look almost the same

S ON LITTLE BIRD LANE

today except the name has changed to Apple Square Apartments, and the street name, Little Bird Lane, has changed to Cedar Street. (Bradshaw's Color Studios, Sedona, Arizona.)

KING'S RANSOM MOTOR HOTEL, C. 1970. This hotel advertised, "Sedona's Newest and finest deluxe units, electric heat, refrigeration, phones, private balconies, a heated swimming pool and T.V. restaurant and lounge, located at 725 Arizona Highway 179." Note all the Mid-Century Modern details. King's Ransom was built on the site of the former Civilian

NSOM MOTOR HOTEL
EK CANYON, ARIZONA

Conservation Corps camp, which later became the Sedona Lodge. At left are signs for Andy Hughes Real Estate. The property was updated recently to a Southwestern style and is currently the Arabella Hotel. (Bradshaw's Color Studios, Sedona, Arizona.)

THE SHRINE OF THE RED ROCKS, C. 1961. This shrine was built by the Masons of Verde Valley and the community of Sedona as a permanent altar for sunrise Easter services. It was dedicated on Easter Sunday 1961 by Sen. Barry Goldwater. The shrine is on Tabletop Mountain, later renamed Airport Mesa as the Sedona Airport continued to grow. (Bradshaw's Color Studios, Sedona, Arizona.)

MASONIC TEMPLE, SEDONA, ARIZONA, C. 1965. The Red Rock Memorial Masonic Lodge No. 63 on Airport Mesa was dedicated on May 15, 1965, as a memorial to William H. Roberts, a York and Scottish Rite Mason. The building remains, but the Masonic Lodge constructed a new facility in Cottonwood, Arizona, in 2019. (Roben Company, Sedona, Arizona.)

ENCHANTMENT RESORT, C. 1988. The Enchantment Resort is located inside beautiful Boyington Canyon on 70 acres of land with breathtaking red rock views, about 10–15 minutes or nine miles west from Uptown Sedona. Enchantment promotes corporate meetings and retreats. The resort consistently receives a 4.5- to 5-star rating for its food and amenities. It offers fitness options, mountain biking, hiking, and indoor and outdoor pools and has five on-site restaurants. Its spa, Mi Amo, offers many services. The resort also offers 18 holes of golf on its nearby private Seven Canyons course. (Bradshaw's Color Studios, Sedona, Arizona.)

Six

The Chapel of the Holy Cross

Chapel of the Holy Cross, c. 1967. The Chapel of the Holy Cross was begun in 1956 by Marguerite Brunswig Staude as a memorial to her parents, Marguerite and Lucien Brunswig. A devout Catholic, Marguerite said she found two symbols on the property that gave her assurance she had found the right location to build a chapel. One was a tall red rock spire that looked like the Madonna holding a child, and the other was an "RX" carved into a rock. Her father, Lucien, made their family fortune creating a chain of drugstores, so she felt that these signs signified her parents' approval. (Bradshaw's Color Studios, Sedona, Arizona.)

LAND FOR THE CHAPEL, C. 1956. The place where Marguerite Brunswig Staude chose to build the chapel was Coconino National Forest land. She used her influence with Arizona senator Barry Goldwater to get her plans reviewed and approved by the state legislature. Goldwater referred to the proposed chapel as "a noble structure." A special use permit was issued. (Petley Studios, Phoenix, Arizona.)

CHAPEL OF THE HOLY CROSS, C. 1959. While there is a widespread belief that the chapel was designed by Frank Lloyd Wright, the design team was Ashen and Allen of San Francisco. The contractor was William Simpson Construction. The ground-breaking and blessing ceremony with the bishop of Santa Fe presiding was held in 1955. (Roben Company, Sedona, Arizona.)

CHAPEL OF THE HOLY CROSS, C. 1959. The chapel was completed in 18 months at a cost of $300,000. Staude stipulated that the doors were open to all for quiet reflection, and no services or weddings were to be held there. She believed that in the modern age, people could experience the spiritual through the power of beauty and art. (Grizzly Feathers, Sedona, Arizona.)

CHAPEL AREA, C. 1959. Formerly known as Little Horse Park, where a number of films were made, this is now called Chapel Area. Marguerite Brunswig Staude gave the chapel to the Spiritual Life of America Institute to administer, but it was later gifted to St. John Vianney Catholic Church of Sedona. Staude stated, "That the church may come to life in the souls of men and be a living reality—herein lies the message of this chapel." (Petley Studios, Phoenix, Arizona.)

CROSS, C. 1958. The chapel was constructed of an aggregate of cement and red stone. The 70-foot-high cross, secured into the red rock, anchors the front of the chapel. The high entrance doors are aluminum, and the door handles are in the shape of communion chalices. In 1957, the American Institute of Architects voted to give the chapel its Award of Honor. (Roben Company, Sedona, Arizona.)

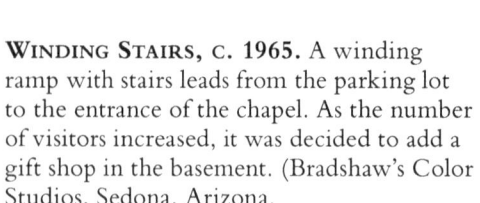

WINDING STAIRS, C. 1965. A winding ramp with stairs leads from the parking lot to the entrance of the chapel. As the number of visitors increased, it was decided to add a gift shop in the basement. (Bradshaw's Color Studios, Sedona, Arizona.

ALTAR, C. 1965. Upon entering the chapel, the eye is immediately drawn to the altar. It is anchored by the cross, with the intention being that the altar and the cross function as one. (Bradshaw's Color Studios, Sedona, Arizona.)

KEITH MUNROE CAST-IRON CROSS, C. 1965. A number of Christian visitors complained about the nontraditional representation of the cross, which was sometimes called "The Christ of the Atomic Age." Complaints that the cross was haunting, shattering, shocking, and a revolting sacrilege continued until it was removed. The artist, Keith Munroe, said that the cross was intended to shock man into thinking. (Bradshaw's Color Studios, Sedona, Arizona.)

CARVED STONE MADONNA, C. 1958. This stone Madonna was carved by Marguerite Brunswig Staude, who had studied stone carving in Mexico. She also created the Stations of the Cross, made of rusty spikes. While it is estimated that the chapel receives millions of visitors each year from all over the world, a respectful meditative silence inside the space is still maintained. In 2005, a Taizé prayer service was instituted and is held each Monday at 5:00 p.m. (Roben Company, Sedona, Arizona.)

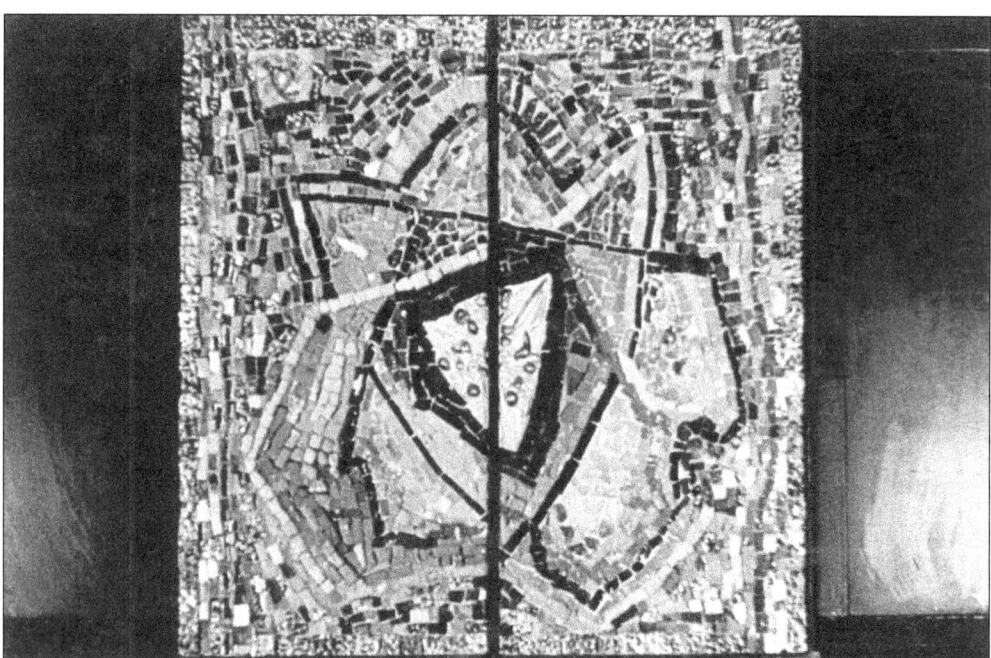

MOSAIC OF TABERNACLE DOOR, C. 1965. Pictured is a modern mosaic by Louisa Jenkins. While changes in the chapel have been made over time, such as a new altar cross and votive candles, Staude's vision to create a place that would "send the spirit onward" has been maintained. (Bradshaw's Color Studios, Sedona, Arizona.)

HERBERT OF THE HOLY CROSS, C. 1969. Herbert, an Australian shepherd, was known as the caretaker's assistant. This image makes for a great, humorous postcard of the Chapel of the Holy Cross. In 2007, the chapel was voted by Arizonans as one of the Seven Man Made Wonders of Arizona. It is listed in the National Register of Historic Places. (Roben Company, Sedona, Arizona.)

ST. JOHN VIANNEY CATHOLIC CHURCH, C. 1965. Located off Route 89A in West Sedona, this church was dedicated on May 11, 1965, by Rev. Bernard T. Espelage, the bishop of Gallup, New Mexico. St. John Vianney maintains wonderful landscaping and gardens around the church that are perfect for spiritual reflection. The church is also responsible for the personnel and maintenance at the Chapel of the Holy Cross. (Roben Company, Sedona, Arizona.)

ST. ANDREW'S EPISCOPAL CHURCH, C. 1971. St. Andrew's Episcopal Church is located at 100 Arroyo Pinion Drive in West Sedona. The church maintains a labyrinth on the lot next door that is open to all who wish to walk in spiritual meditation. (Bradshaw's Color Studios, Sedona, Arizona.)

INTERIOR OF ST. ANDREW'S EPISCOPAL CHURCH, C. 1971. St. Andrew's mission statement reads, "Whatever your religious background, and however you have come to be here with us, we welcome you. We hope that you will feel comforted and fulfilled and that through worship and fellowship, you will be strengthened to meet the challenges of your daily lives. We would love to welcome you into this community of faith. All are welcome. Come as you are." (Bradshaw's Color Studios, Sedona, Arizona.)

CHRIST LUTHERAN CHURCH, SEDONA, C. 1971. This church is on the corner of Chapel Road and Route 179. "It's God's Work, Our Hands" is the mission statement of this Evangelical Lutheran Church in America church, and it is recognized for its support of Verde Valley food banks and other community projects. The church also has an excellent music program and sponsors free concerts for the community. (Peter L. Bloomer photograph, Sedona, Arizona.)

BEAUTIFUL RED ROCK PINNACLES, C. 1965. Fall is a quieter time in Oak Creek Canyon, with a riot of beautiful colors. Many people visit the area seeking inner peace, spiritual reflection, and new directions by observing the beauty of nature all around them. (Bradshaw's Color Studios, Sedona, Arizona.)

Seven
OAK CREEK CANYON

WILSON CANYON BRIDGE, C. 1938. Located north of Uptown Sedona leading into lower Oak Creek Canyon, this bridge was first named Wilson Canyon Bridge because it spanned Wilson Canyon. The 200-foot-long steel arch bridge was built by Lewis Brothers of Phoenix and dedicated by Arizona governor Rawghlie Clement Stanford, state senator James Babbitt, Maj. W.W. Midgley, and six local musical groups. (Albertype Company, Brooklyn, New York.)

WILSON CANYON BRIDGE, OAK CREEK CANYON, ARIZONA, REAL-PHOTO POSTCARD, C. 1945. When first built, the bridge carried Route 179, but later the highway was renamed by the Arizona Department of Transportation to 89A. In 1984, it was designated a scenic road. The bridge was also renamed Midgley Bridge in honor of Maj. W.W. Midgley, a local rancher and businessman who had been a strong advocate for constructing the bridge and building good roads in Arizona. (Publisher unidentified.)

MIDGLEY BRIDGE OVER WILSON CREEK, OAK CREEK, ARIZONA, C. 1945. Midgely Bridge is on Route 89A, which connects the towns of Flagstaff, Sedona, and Jerome and climbs the Mingus Mountains into Prescott. The bridge was listed in the National Register of Historic Places in 1989. (Curteich, Chicago, Illinois.)

OAK CREEK CANYON, HIGHWAY 89A, REAL-PHOTO POSTCARD, C. 1948. Oak Creek Canyon Road 89A runs through Coconino National Forest and has 18 miles of spectacular beauty. It has often been called the most beautiful 18 miles in Arizona. The elevation ranges from 4,000 feet at the northern edge of Sedona to 7,000 feet at the top of the switchbacks. (Publisher unidentified.)

OAK CREEK AT INDIAN GARDENS, REAL-PHOTO POSTCARD, C. 1945. Native Americans, perhaps the Sinagua or Yavapai Apaches, discovered that a flat area in Oak Creek Canyon was the perfect place to farm beans and squash, but then the soldiers at Camp Verde removed the Indians to the San Carlos Indian Reservation. When J.J. Thomson, thought to be the first Anglo settler to come to the Indian Gardens area, arrived in 1876, some say he found a garden that Indians had planted and named the area after them. Thompson raised nine children on the property and is credited with building the first road from Indian Gardens to the area that became the town of Sedona. A historic marker was placed on the east side of Indian Gardens to recognize his contributions. (Publisher unidentified.)

INDIAN GARDENS, C. 1954. In addition to the Texaco service station and café/fountain, a dance hall was built in Indian Gardens in 1931–1932 and was famous for the midnight to sunrise dances held there. The building was also used as a skating rink. (Color Roundup Photo Shop, Sedona, Arizona.)

INDIAN GARDENS, C. 1958. A new building has been added between the café/fountain and skating rink, and the expanded market has a large new sign. The skating rink was purchased by the US Forest Service and torn down in 1974 for parking, but the rock building is still a café. (Bradshaw's Photo Shop, Sedona, Arizona.)

ROADWAY THROUGH OAK CREEK CANYON, REAL-PHOTO POSTCARD, C. 1958. Travelers enjoy views of the red canyon walls and pines, which form a beautiful contrast against the red rocks and blue skies. (Petley Studios, Phoenix, Arizona.)

TODD'S LODGE, OAK CREEK CANYON, REAL-PHOTO POSTCARD, C. 1948. In 1927, Todd and Catherine McIlwee bought a 10-acre parcel in Oak Creek Canyon. The land had been the original 1908 homestead of Jesse "Bear" Howard, who had the bad luck of meeting a big bear. Miners from Jerome came to fish in Oak Creek, and word spread about Catherine McIlwee's good cooking. A woman is sitting and enjoying the spectacular view of the Oak Creek Canyon cliffs. (Publisher unidentified.)

TODD'S LODGE, OAK CREEK CANYON, C. 1963. The McIlwees and their son Todd built four cabins and added a dining room in 1936. Todd Jr. and his wife raised four daughters at the lodge. The lush grass lawns, flower gardens, and magnificent views were lovely, but the big attraction continued to be the chicken dinners, from chickens raised on the property, coupled with apples, pears, plums, peaches, fresh vegetables, and homemade cakes and pies. (Bradshaw's Color Studios, Sedona, Arizona.)

TODD'S LODGE GARDENS, C. 1967. Another great feature of a stay at Todd's Lodge was that the location was off Route 89A west of Oak Creek and could only be accessed by a private road. Radio service used to be spotty in the canyon, and no televisions or phones were installed in the cabins, leaving plenty of time for strolling the beautiful gardens and relaxing. By 1970, the Todd family had welcomed guests every Easter through Thanksgiving, and were ready to retire. Todd's Lodge was sold to Sedona developer Abe Miller, who sold it in 1972 to Bill and Georgiana Garland. (Bob Bradshaw, Sedona, Arizona.)

GARLAND'S, OAK CREEK LODGE, C. 1970. Bill and Georgiana Garland renovated the cabins and main building, but decided to leave a portion of the original log cabin in the kitchen. The management was turned over to their son Bill and his wife, Mary, in 1972. They promised to continue the American plan of lodging, and also promised that the practice of growing food on the property and having the highest standards of cooking and serving would not change. The family diversified into selling Indian arts, rugs, and jewelry at their Indian Gardens and Sedona stores. In 2014, the lodge was sold. It is now Orchard Canyon Lodge. (Bradshaw's Color Studios, Sedona, Arizona.)

DON HOEL'S CABINS IN THE HEART OF OAK CREEK CANYON, C. 1963. Don Hoel and his wife, Nina, moved from Glendale to purchase 11 primitive cabins in 1945 on the land that was homesteaded by pioneer John L.V. Thomas. Don renovated the cabins and added 15 more. The Hoels were advocates of bringing electricity to Oak Creek Canyon in the late 1940s. They advertised 24 scenic points of interest within reach of Oak Creek Canyon, plus trout fishing, swimming, hiking, horseback riding, painting, photography, and reading. (Publisher unidentified.)

DON HOEL'S CABINS, C. 1965. Business at Don Hoel's was increasing, so Hoel added a grocery store, fishing supplies, and Chevron gas pumps. He worked continuously on improving the cabins, and the demand to stay there constantly increased. (Fronske Studio, Flagstaff, Arizona.)

DON HOEL'S CABINS, C. 1969. Native Americans routinely came through Oak Creek Canyon to gather plants, wild celery, and other herbs. They asked Don Hoel to buy or trade supplies for their rugs, baskets, kachinas, and jewelry. Hoel had a great eye for Native American arts and crafts, and what began as a few items on a shelf became a thriving business. (Bradshaw's Color Studios, Sedona, Arizona.)

DON HOEL'S CABINS, C. 1970. By 1970, the Hoels had hired a manager for the cabins and store, and built a home and opened Hoel's Indian Shop, which Don's grandson continues to operate. When Don and Nina Hoel passed, the property was sold in 2006. Don Hoel's officially closed on November 29, 2006. The new owner proposed a rezoning for 11 building lots in 2008. However, the property became the Butterfly Garden Inn in 2018 and is a popular place for weddings and other events. (Bradshaw's Color Roundup.)

CALL OF THE CANYON RESORT, OAK CREEK CANYON, REAL-PHOTO POSTCARD, C. 1945. Call of the Canyon Resort in Oak Creek Canyon had cottages, gasoline, and groceries. The single gas pump is a Union 76 visible pump, and on the other side of the entryway is a Coca-Cola sign. The lodge was named for the popular Western novel *Call of the Canyon*, written in 1921 by Zane Grey, and for the silent film of the same name filmed in Oak Creek Canyon in 1923, starring Richard Dix, Lois Wilson, and Marjorie Daw. (Frasher's Fotos, Pomona, California.)

CALL OF THE CANYON RESORT, REAL-PHOTO POSTCARD, C. 1944. Call of the Canyon was located in upper Oak Creek. Zane Grey is believed to have written portions of *Call of the Canyon* while staying at Mayhew's Oak Creek Lodge, Lolomi Lodge, and the Weatherford Hotel in Flagstaff. (Frasher's Fotos, Pomona, California.)

CALL OF THE CANYON RESORT, C. 1956. Call of the Canyon was 19 miles south of Flagstaff on Route 89A. The altitude is 5,329. A 1950s square gas pump has replaced the older visible gas pump. (Bradshaw's Color Studios, Sedona, Arizona.)

CALL OF THE CANYON RESORT, C. 1963. The back of this card reads, "Relax here for the rest of your life in Upper Oak Creek Canyon where it's cool. You'll find spacious comfortable cabins, a refreshing swimming pool and gracious hospitality." (Petley Studios, Phoenix, Arizona.)

CALL OF THE CANYON SWIMMING POOL, C. 1968. This swimming pool was 125 feet by 50 feet, and was the largest pool in northern Arizona at the time it was built. A diver stands poised on the diving stand while two teenaged girls are sunbathing. (Bradshaw's Color Studios, Sedona, Arizona.)

JUNIPINE, OAK CREEK CANYON, REAL-PHOTO POSTCARD, C. 1948. F.M. Gold bought property about 1.8 miles north of Slide Rock in 1926 and built a store and cabins on land that had been part of the original 1800s Purtyman homestead. The name Junipine was chosen for two intertwining juniper pines on the property that appeared as one tree. At the time of this photograph, Junipine had a small grocery store and Chevron gas pumps. Note the small sign below the Chevron sign advertising apples. (Publisher unidentified.)

JUNIPINE CABINS, C. 1969. In front of the store are Mobil gas pumps, a sign advertising the cabins, signs for film, maps, groceries, and a Bell telephone booth. The Junipine now has a restaurant with indoor and outdoor seating. Today, the cabins/houses are individually owned. (Roben Company, Sedona, Arizona; photograph by Rollie F. Houck.)

MAYHEW'S OAK CREEK LODGE, C. 1963. Ethel Mayhew's reputation for her special trout and pies became well known, and the Mayhews' guest register was impressive. Pres. Herbert Hoover was a guest, as well as Walt Disney and movie stars Clark Gable, Caesar Romero, Maureen O'Hara, and Jimmy Stewart. During the summer months, the Mayhew family worked up to 18 hours a day, but the lodge closed during the winter due to a lack of central heating. Eventually, Ethel sold the lodge in 1968 to the US Forest Service for a visitor center, but it burned before any renovations could be made. Hikers on the West Fork Trail comment on the foundation and the chimney that remain. (Bradshaw's Color Studios, Sedona, Arizona.)

OAK CREEK LODGE (LATER MAYHEW'S LODGE), REAL-PHOTO POSTCARD, C. 1945. The lodge began as a rustic cabin built by pioneer "Bear" Howard around 1880. In 1925, Carl and Ethel Mayhew bought the 40-acre property and built another cabin for their home. It was primitive, without running water or electricity. The lodge mainly catered to fishermen and hunters. Later, they combined the two cabins and added a second story for a total of 10 bedrooms. They also built a swimming pool. The name changed from Oak Creek Lodge to Mayhew's Lodge. This postcard is rare and expensive. (Publisher unidentified.)

CHIPMUNK STORE AND CABINS, UPPER OAK CREEK CANYON, ARIZONA, REAL-PHOTO POSTCARD, C. 1949. The Chipmunk Store and Cabins were built on the former Harding homestead in Upper Oak Creek, about 12 miles north of Sedona. A Shell gas pump sits in front of the store. Unfortunately, the Chipmunk burned in 1977. (Publisher unidentified.)

FLOOD'S CHIPMUNK LODGE, C. 1962. The Chipmunk Store and Cabins were purchased by Ethel and Bill Flood in April 1954. They updated the store and cabin and sold sandwiches, short orders, and homemade pies and cakes. It is not hard to imagine guests sitting in the metal motel chairs out front enjoying the view of the cliffs or the passing traffic on Route 89A. They also sold soft drinks and beer. Note the A-1 Beer sign. A-1 was brewed in Phoenix. The Shell visible gas pump remained. (Bradshaw's Color Roundup, Sedona, Arizona.)

OAK CREEK, OAK CREEK CANYON, ARIZONA, REAL-PHOTO POSTCARD, C. 1952. It is hard to spot the fisherman or hikers or those cooling their feet in Oak Creek due to the massive size of the canyon walls. Oak Creek is often called Live Oak Creek because it runs continuously all year. (Publisher unidentified.)

WINTER BRINGS AN ADDED TOUCH OF BEAUTY, 1965. Oak Creek Canyon has a different type of beauty in the winter months when it snows. Lower Oak Creek Canyon trees have shed their foliage, allowing visitors to see cabins and rock formations that are not visible during summer months. Upper Oak Creek becomes a destination for visitors to photograph the frosted rocks and trees. (Bradshaw Distributing Company, Sedona, Arizona.)

SWITCHBACKS IN OAK CREEK CANYON, REAL-PHOTO POSTCARD, C. 1948. Route 89A climbs north toward Flagstaff from about 4,000 feet in Uptown Sedona to 7,000 feet at the top of Oak Creek Canyon. After leaving the Silver Spring Fish Hatchery in Upper Oak Creek Canyon, 89A begins to climb higher along a series of switchbacks. Today, the highway has been widened and has guardrails, but for "flatlanders," driving or riding up the winding switchbacks to Oak Creek Vista at the top can be challenging. (Publisher unidentified.)

FAMOUS OAK CREEK CANYON SWITCHBACKS, C. 1969. On the 2.5-mile portion of Route 89A through Oak Creek Canyon, called the Switchbacks, there are seven curving levels. (Petley Studios, Phoenix, Arizona.)

TOUR BUS ON OAK CREEK CANYON SWITCHBACKS, C. 1950. According to the back of this card, "The ride through Oak Creek Canyon is one of Arizona's most colorful trips, with Oak Creek winding along below and precipitous red rock walls towering above the highway." (Curteich Chicago, Illinois.)

OAK CREEK CANYON, ARIZONA, C. 1965. During any season of the year, the views in Oak Creek Canyon are beautiful. The tall cliffs of red and white limestone dotted with pines are always present. In the fall, the maples, aspens, and oaks provide a red and yellow color show. During winter, when some of the trees have lost their leaves, one can notice buildings and rocks that are obscured during spring and summer. In spring, the wildflower blossoms and spring greens of the new leaves are beautiful. During summer, the lush vegetation and wildflowers have grown, and sitting by the creek is a refreshing place to spend time. (Dick Parrish, Phoenix, Arizona.)

UPPER OAK CREEK CANYON, ARIZONA, C. 1946. This postcard was mailed from Flagstaff in 1946 with a 1¢ stamp. It is always fun to read the back of postcards to get an idea of what the sender had to say about the area. The most common words on the back of Sedona or Oak Creek cards are "fun," "beautiful," "colorful," "scenic," and "sunshine." (Publisher unidentified.)

Eight
RECREATION SEDONA STYLE

FISHIN' TIME IN OAK CREEK CANYON, C. 1962. In the early years, Oak Creek Canyon attracted hunters of bear, deer, and mountain lions, but once the area was settled, fishing for German browns and other varieties of trout became one of the area's most popular sports. (Bradshaw Distributing Company, Sedona, Arizona.)

LANDING THE BIG ONES IN OAK CREEK, C. 1957. Old-timers talk about the rainbow trout they caught in Oak Creek using worms, crickets, grasshoppers, and standard spinners. Many of the early lodges in Oak Creek Canyon cleaned and cooked their guests' fish. The Sterling Fish Hatchery still transfers minnows to the hatcheries in Page Springs, then returns to stock them in Oak Creek. (Bradshaw's Photo Shop, Sedona, Arizona.)

SWIMMING POOL AT CALL OF THE CANYON RESORT, C. 1942. The swimming pool and diving stand in Oak Creek Canyon is crowded with swimmers at Call of the Canyon Resort on Route 89A. As proclaimed on the back of this card, "The ideal place for your vacations." (Curteich, Chicago, Illinois.)

SWIMMING POOL AT CALL OF THE CANYON RESORT, C. 1960. The swimming pool at Call of the Canyon Resort was the largest pool in northern Arizona at 125 feet by 50 feet. Here, umbrellas have been added for shade, but because more resorts and hotels had built swimming pools by this time, the pool was less crowded. (Bradshaw's Color Studio, Sedona, Arizona.)

DEVIL'S ARCH, C. 1959. Hiking has long been a favorite activity of visitors and residents alike. Devil's Arch Trail is one of the most popular hiking trails to the natural sandstone bridge. The arch can be accessed by hiking from Dry Creek Road in West Sedona. The hike is about one mile from the Dry Creek parking area. There are stunning views from the top of the arch if a hiker is not afraid of heights. Views can be seen from the bottom of the arch, too. (Roben Company, Sedona, Arizona.)

BELL ROCK AND COURTHOUSE HIKING TRAILS, C. 1955. Bell Rock and Courthouse Trails offer longer hikes around both formations as well as shorter hikes. Climbing on Bell Rock is a favorite of hikers, but the rocks can be slippery when wet. Also, climbing up Bell Rock must be easier than climbing down, as several hikers are rescued off Bell Rock each year. There is a parking area to the south, Bell Rock Vista, and another to the north, Courthouse Vista, where trail information is posted. Other popular trails include Wilson Trail on the north side of Midgley Bridge, and West Fork, a three-mile hike in Oak Creek Canyon. A trail for more advanced hikers is the Sterling Pass Trail in Oak Creek Canyon, which climbs in a corkscrew fashion to the top of the ridge. (Rembrandt Post Card, Nobel Inc., Colorado Springs, Colorado.)

OAK CREEK CANYON, C. 1945. Birding in Oak Creek Canyon was and still is an activity many people enjoy. Birds include blue jays, cardinals, hepatic tanagers, summer tanagers, hawks, and great horned owls. In the summer, people enjoy picking wild berries and foraging. Camping, picnicking, and bicycling in Oak Creek Canyon continue to be popular. (Curteich, Chicago, Illinois.)

SLIDE ROCK, OAK CREEK CANYON, C. 1968. The 286 acres of the former Pendley homestead farm, where Slide Rock, formerly named Oak Creek Falls, is located, were purchased by the Arizona Park Lands Fund in February 1983 for $3.5 million to become Slide Rock State Park. A visitor center, restrooms, and a parking lot were built. The parking lot alleviated cars parking along Route 89A and pedestrians crossing the two-lane road. Red Rock State Park opened in July 1987 as a day-use park. While some complained about the park collecting a fee for an area that used to be free and limiting the hours of use, Slide Rock is now a cleaner and safer place to have fun. (Petley Studios, Phoenix, Arizona.)

POCO DIABLO GOLF CLUB AND RESTAURANT, C. 1969. Before the Poco Diablo Resort was built, a nine-hole golf course, clubhouse, restaurant, and cocktail lounge run by Dick and June Duncan was operating off Route 179. The Poco Diablo Resort, which includes tennis courts, was built around the golf course. (Bradshaw's Color Studios, Sedona, Arizona.)

SADDLE ROCK GUEST RANCH, C. 1962. The Saddle Rock Guest Ranch is now a bed-and-breakfast for six guests in West Sedona off Route 89A. The property was the former Cook Ranch, built in 1926. The ranch has been updated but still retains its original fireplace, flagstone floors, and Ponderosa pine ceiling beams. The swimming, horseback riding, hunting, fishing, and excellent food keep guests returning. Famous guests who stayed there include John Wayne, Jimmy Stewart, and Orson Wells. Sugar Loaf Mountain can be seen in the background. (Dexter Press Inc., West Nyack, New York; photograph by Bob Bradshaw.)

PINTO RIDING STABLES, SEDONA, ARIZONA, C. 1967. Horses could be rented by the hour or day for the forest trails around Sedona or in Oak Creek Canyon. Evening cookouts or breakfast trail rides, wagon rides, or hayrides could be arranged. (Roben Company, Sedona, Arizona.)

HORSEBACK RIDING, SEDONA, ARIZONA, C. 1965. Three riders pause to admire the views of red rock formations. During this period, there were a few open areas in Sedona that still had spaces for horses. (Bradshaw's Photo Shop, Sedona, Arizona.)

VACATION LAND OF NORTHERN ARIZONA, C. 1967. Printed on the back of this card is "Cool Pine Forests—Trout Water—Breathtaking Scenery." In 1967, these riders show that Sedona and Oak Creek Canyon still retained their Western image. In fact, one of the most popular restaurants was called the Ranch House, but Sedona would soon favor a more sophisticated vibe. (Bradshaw's Color Studios, Sedona, Arizona.)

Jeep Tours into rugged back cour

Don Pratt Jeep Tours, c. 1969. Don Pratt was once a Hollywood and Las Vegas musician who moved to Sedona to start a real estate business. He began using his Jeep for his real estate business, and since he loved the backcountry around Sedona, he would sometimes take his customers out into areas where most cars could not go. Customers loved the Jeeps and the backcountry, and Pratt soon realized that experiencing Sedona by Jeep would be a great

in spectacular Oak Creek Canyon

business. He got a big break when an executive from Eastman Kodak took one of his Jeep tours and began promoted the Jeeps as a great way to photograph the spectacular scenery. When Pratt sold the business, the name was changed to Pink Jeep tours. The tours were so popular that several other Jeep tour companies began operating. Hummer, ATV, and helicopter tours would come later. (Kolor View Press, Los Angeles, California.)

WINTERTIME IN OAK CREEK CANYON, C. 1965. When January arrives and most of the country is trying to escape snow, a snowfall in Sedona is cause for crazy driving and building snowmen. When the television stations in Phoenix report snow in Sedona, Oak Creek Canyon, and Flagstaff, the roads are jammed with people from central and southern Arizona. (Bradshaw Distributing Company, Sedona, Arizona.)

Nine
MISCELLANEOUS

VERDE VALLEY PREPARATORY SCHOOL, C. 1966. Barbara and Hamilton Warren moved from Boston to Big Park, which would become the village of Oak Creek, and bought 200 acres to start a school to foster international and intercultural understanding. They opened the school in 1948 with 16 students of high academic standards. The school continues to operate and still attracts international and domestic students with high academic standards. (Bradshaw's Photo Shop, Sedona, Arizona.)

BIRDS AND ANIMALS OF OAK CREEK CANYON AND NORTHERN ARIZONA, C. 1968. Various birds like king fisher, green violet swallow, white throated swift, western tanager, yellow warbler, blue grossbeak, water quzel, and stellar jays are found around Oak Creek Canyon and northern Arizona. There are also a variety of animals, such as grey squirrel, mule deer, mountain lion, coyote, bobcat, abert squirrel, raccoon, grey fox, skunk, porcupine, ringtail cat, and chipmunk. The bears that were found in Oak Creek Canyon in the early years were pushed to higher elevations as development increased. (Roben Company, Sedona, Arizona.)

PROSPECTOR AND DONKEYS PASS THROUGH OAK CREEK, C. 1965. Mining has always been a part of the area surrounding Sedona, from the salt mines near Camp Verde to the copper mines in Jerome. At one time, a large mining company was negotiating to purchase the beautiful area that is Red Rock State Park today. Fortunately, the company's offer was not approved. (Dexter Press Inc., West Nyack, New York.)

OAK CREEK CANARIES, C. 1965. This herd of shaggy burros, one of the most useful pack animals, stands in front of a watering hole with Oak Creek Canyon in the background. Miners sometimes called burros "canaries." (Bradshaw Distributing Company, Sedona, Arizona.)

SNOOPY ON THE ROCKS, C. 1960. Pictured is an unidentified artist's rendition of comic strip dog Snoopy on top of his doghouse. Charles Schultz created *Peanuts* in 1950. Snoopy Rock is part of the larger Camelhead Rock formation. (Roben Company, Sedona, Arizona.)

SANTA GOING DOWN CHIMNEY ROCK, C. 1960. This unidentified artist's Christmas card shows Santa with his sack of presents going down Chimney Rock. (Roben Company, Sedona, Arizona.)

Tlaquepaque Arts and Crafts Village, Sedona, Arizona, 1979. Tlaquepaque (an Indian word meaning "the best of everything") Arts and Crafts Village on Route 179 was built by Sedona developer Abe Miller. He envisioned a village in the Spanish Colonial style that would resemble a small village in Mexico, with shops featuring arts and crafts and fine restaurants. Miller hired architect Robert McIntyre to travel to Mexico with him to take pictures for ideas and to search for items that fit his vision for Tlaquepaque. McIntyre made sure that the buildings were not exactly square or plum to create the illusion that they had been built over a long period of time. Tlaquepaque remains popular with both residents and visitors and has expanded across Route 179 to the area called Tlaquepaque North. Many special events such as farmer's markets, Mexican fiestas, chili cook-offs, Christmas celebrations, concerts, and others take place at Tlaquepaque. The popularity of the fine restaurants, diverse galleries, and shops as well as the beauty of the old trees have made Abe Miller's vision of Tlaquepaque a reality. (Bradshaw's Color Studios, Sedona, Arizona.)

TLAQUEPAQUE VILLAGE FRONT VIEW, 1979. The property next to Oak Creek where Tlaquepaque was built was the land that T. Carl and Sedona Schnebly had owned years before. A variety of wonderful old Sycamore trees were saved and incorporated into the design of the project. The ground-breaking ceremony was held in 1971. Items from Mexico, such as iron railings and gates, doors, tiles, lanterns, benches, fountains, and other design elements, were incorporated into the plans. The shops, galleries, restaurants, courtyards, and a small chapel for meditation were completed in 1978. (Bradshaw's Color Studios, Sedona, Arizona.)

BIBLIOGRAPHY

Benore, Loretta. *History, Hilarity and Heartbreak: Sedona Stories and More.* Sedona, AZ: Sedona Heritage Publishing, 2016.

Bradshaw, Bob. *The Sedona Man: The Life and Adventures of Arizona Cowboy Bob Bradshaw.* Sedona, AZ: Bradshaw Enterprises, 2002.

———. "They Still Go Thisaway and Thataway in the Red Rock Country." *Arizona Highways.* May 1959: 6–9.

Heidinger, Lisa Schnebly, Janeen Trevillyan, and the Sedona Historical Society. *Sedona.* Charleston, SC: Arcadia Publishing, 2007.

Sedona Westerners. *Those Early Days: A Pioneer History of Sedona and Vicinity.* Sedona-Oak Creek, AZ: Sedona Heritage Publishing, Rev. 2008.

Slade, R.J. "A Bell for Sedona." *Arizona Highways.* May 1959: 2–5.

Wood, Dr. Harry. "Sedona's Unique Mexican Village of Arts and Crafts." *Arizona Highways.* May 1981: 38–44.

Visit us at
arcadiapublishing.com

www.ingramcontent.com/pod-product-compliance
Lightning Source LLC
Chambersburg PA
CBHW060938170426
43194CB00027B/2989